My birthday

1

Numbers and colours

1 Read. Then colour.

1 pink

2 purple

3 orange

4 brown

5 black

6 white

7 grey

2 Read, look and match.

a

b

c

d

1 walk
2 run
3 stamp
4 climb
5 jump
6 dance
7 clap
8 hop

e

f

g

h

3 Trace and colour.

1 butterfly

2 bird

3 flower

4 fish

1 What's your name?

4 Read. Then complete.

1
What's your **name**?

Sally

2
_____ your name?

Tommy

3
_____ name?
My name's Debbie.

Debbie

4
_____ Fred.

Fred

5 Read. Then write and colour the cakes.

How old are you? What's your favourite colour?

1

I'm eight. __My__ favourite colour __is__ pink.

2

I'm ten. My _____ colour _____ yellow.

3

I'm three. _____ _____ _____ purple.

6 Write for you. Then draw and colour.

How old are you? What's your favourite colour?

I'm _____ _____ _____ _____ .

7 Unscramble. Then write.

1

name Tim . My is

My name is Tim.

2

red ? it Is

3

it What ? is colour

4

are old ? you How

8 Read. Then match.

1

What colour

a

isn't.

2

Is it

b

green.

3

No, it

c

purple?

4

It's

d

is it?

9 Read. Then colour.

Hello Tom,

It's my birthday today. I'm seven.
How old are you? My birthday cake
is brown with seven purple candles.
My favourite colour is purple!
What's your favourite colour?

From
Emma

10 Read and circle.

1 How old is Emma?   (seven) / eight

2 What is Emma's favourite colour?   brown / purple

3 Is the cake orange?   yes / no

4 What colour are Emma's candles?   purple / pink

1 A letter

Remember!

Names **start with a** capital letter.

Sentences **start with a** capital letter.

His name is Tom. He's eight.

11 Read and circle.

1 (my / My) favourite colour is red.

2 (The / the) butterfly is yellow.

3 (it's / It's) my birthday today.

4 Tom is eight and (emma / Emma) is seven.

12 Write. Use words from the box.

| eight | ~~Emma~~ | orange | From | birthday |

Hello ¹___Emma___ ,

Today is my ²_____.

I'm ³_____.

My favourite colour is

⁴_____.

⁵_____ Tom

At school

What's this?

1 **Look and read. Then circle.**

1 (book) / pencil

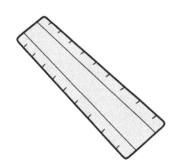

2 ruler / rubber

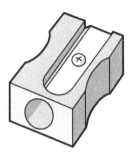

3 pen / pencil sharpener

4 pen / pencil case

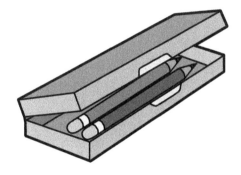

5 pencil case / chair

6 desk / rubber

2 **Read. Then write.**

fifteen   seventeen   ~~eleven~~   nineteen   fourteen

eleven , twelve, thirteen, _____ , _____ sixteen,
_____ , eighteen, _____ , twenty

2 What are these?

3 Read and circle. Then draw and colour.

1 What are (*this* / *these*)?

They (*'s* / *are*) blue pencils.

2 What (*is* / *are*) this?

It (*'s* / *are*) a brown desk.

3 What are (*this* / *these*)?

(*It* / *They*) are red pens.

4 What (*is* / *are*) this?

It (*'s* / *are*) a ruler.

What colour (*is* / *are*) it?

It (*'s* / *are*) green.

4 Look and trace the word. Then write the number.

1 How many pianos can you see?

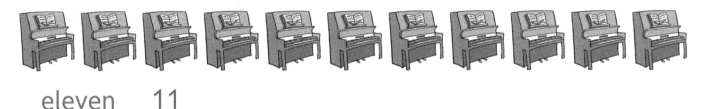

eleven   11

2 How many guitars can you see?

fifteen

3 How many drums can you see?

thirteen

4 How many violins can you see?

twelve

2 How many ...?

5 Look, read and complete.

| can | four | ~~many~~ | five |

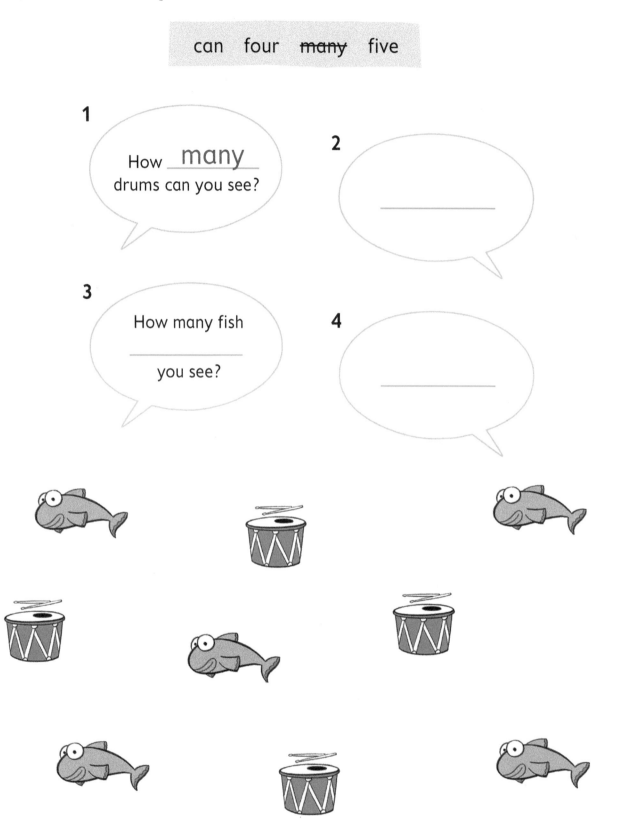

1 How __many__ drums can you see?

2 _____

3 How many fish _____ you see?

4 _____

6 Read. Then trace and draw.

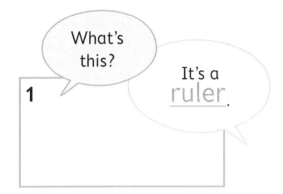

1 What's this? It's a ruler.

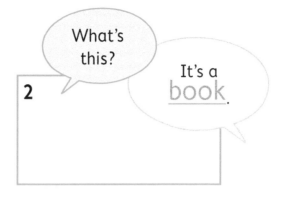

2 What's this? It's a book.

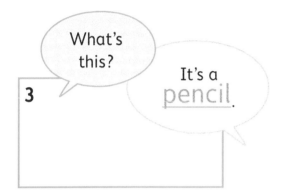

3 What's this? It's a pencil.

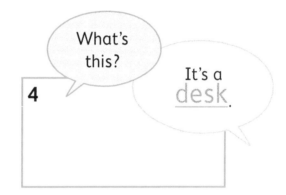

4 What's this? It's a desk.

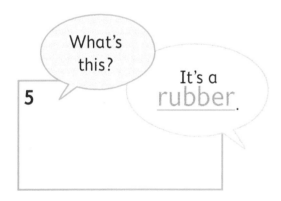

5 What's this? It's a rubber.

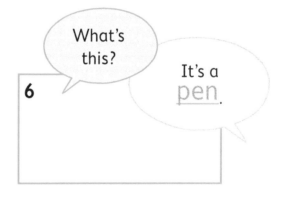

6 What's this? It's a pen.

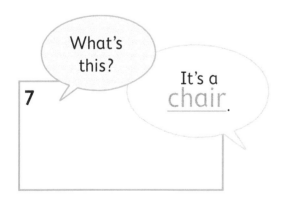

7 What's this? It's a chair.

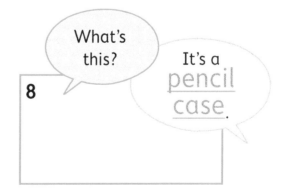

8 What's this? It's a pencil case.

2 Describing a room

Remember!

they're = they are

it's = it is

7 Read and write. Use *they're* and *it's*.

1 They are tables.

   <u>They're tables.</u>

2 It is a drum.

   _____

3 They are my favourite instruments.

   _____

4 It is red and white. What is it?

   _____

5 They are red.

   _____

6 It is a yellow book.

   _____

8 Find and count. Then trace.

1 <u>rubbers</u> | 4 |

2 <u>pencils</u> | |

3 <u>rulers</u> | |

4 <u>books</u> | |

My family **3**
Jobs

1 Unscramble. Then write the family members.

1 mmu ___mum___

2 oetrrhb _____

3 add _____

4 eissrt _____

5 nyagnr _____

6 ddnrgaa _____

2 Look and match.

1 vet

2 doctor

3 artist

4 pilot

5 farmer

6 cook

3 Look, read and match.

1 collage

2 sculpture

3 painting

4 drawing

a

b

c

d

4 Unscramble. Then write.

1

| brother | is | This | my | . |

This _____

2

| old | How | ? | he | is |

_____

3

| ten | . | He | 's |

_____

4

| is | This | . | sister | my |

_____

5

| 's | . | seven | She |

_____

5 Look and write. Use words from the box.

No   Is   ~~she~~   is   Yes   he   No

1

Is <u>she</u> a cook?
_____, she isn't.

2

Is she a cook?
Yes, she _____.

3

_____ he a pilot?
_____, he isn't.

4

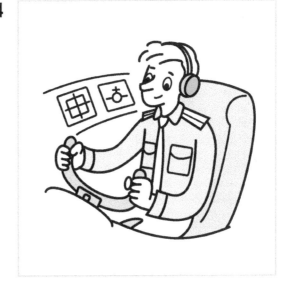

Is _____ a pilot?
_____, he is.

6 **Look and read. Then circle.**

	artist	doctor	cook	farmer	vet
Mum	✗	✗	✗	✗	✔
Dad	✗	✔	✗	✗	✗
Granny	✔	✗	✔	✗	✗
Grandad	✗	✗	✗	✔	✗

1 Is Mum a vet?   Yes, she is. / No, she isn't.

2 Is Grandad a cook?   Yes he is. / No, he isn't.

3 Is Dad a doctor?   Yes, he is. / No, he isn't.

4 Is Granny a farmer?   Yes, she is. / No, she isn't.

7 **Draw a person in your family. Then write.**

This is my _____.

Is _____ an artist?

_____.

8 **Read. Then trace and number.**

1 Hello, I'm Matthew.

I'm seven.

This is my family.

2 This is my brother.

He's eleven.

3 This is my sister.

She's eight.

4 This is my mum.

5 And this is my dad.

9 **Draw your family. Then write.**

Hello, I'm _____.

I'm _____. This is my family.

_____

_____

_____

_____

_____

_____

_____

_____

Remember!

We use a ? after a question. We use a . after a sentence.

Is your mum a vet? No, she isn't.

10 **Read and write.**

1 Is she a vet?

No, she isn't.
She's a farmer.

2 Is she a teacher?

_____

_____

3 Is she an artist?

_____

_____

4 Is he a cook?

_____

_____

5 Is he a doctor?

_____

_____

6 Is he a farmer?

_____

_____

11 **Circle and write. Then draw.**

My (*mum / dad*) is

_____.

body / clothes

1 Unscramble. Then write and match.

1 ckoss   s o c k s

2 rsTthi   _ - _ _ _ _ _

3 sseoh   _ _ _ _ _

4 eotssrru   _ _ _ _ _ _ _ _

5 tha   _ _ _

6 riskt   _ _ _ _ _

7 jmrupe   _ _ _ _ _ _

2 Look, read and write.

arms   legs   ~~fingers~~   body

1 I've got six _____fingers_____ .

2 I've got three _____ .

3 I've got four _____ .

4 I've got one _____ .

I've got two arms

3 Read and match. Then write.

1  **2** 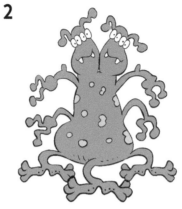 **3**

a

I've got three legs.
I've got two heads.
I've got eight eyes.

b

I've got one head.
I've got two eyes.
I've got three legs.

c

_____

_____

_____

_____

_____

4 Read. Look at Activity 1. Then write (✔) or (✘).

1 I'm monster 1.
I've got four eyes, three arms and four toes. ☐

2 I'm monster 2.
I've got two heads, eight eyes and three legs. ☐

3 I'm monster 3.
I've got nine fingers, four legs and two wings. ☐

5 **Unscramble and write. Then draw.**

| green | He's | heads | two | got |

1 _____.

| got | fingers | eight | blue | He's |

2 _____.

| three | three | She's | feet | got | legs | and |

3 _____.

1

2		3

4 She's got ...

6 **Look and write. Then draw. Use the table.**

(I've)	(got (a))	(green)	jumper
		(yellow)	(trousers)
She's	got (a)	purple	dress
		red	skirt
			shoes
He's	got (a)	black	socks
		pink	(hat)

1 I've got green trousers and a yellow hat.

2 She's _____

3 He's _____

7 Read. Then draw and colour.

Hi, I'm Jenny. This is my brother.
His name is Ben. He's eight.
He's got brown eyes and blond hair.
Look at his favourite clothes!
He's got a red and blue T-shirt.
He's got green shorts and he's got brown
and white shoes.

8 Read. Then circle *Yes* or *No*.

1	This is Ben.	(Yes) / No
2	Ben's got blue eyes.	Yes / No
3	Ben is nine.	Yes / No
4	Ben's got brown and white shorts.	Yes / No
5	Ben's got a red and blue T-shirt.	Yes / No

9 Read. Then draw and colour.

1 He's got clean hands.   **2** She's got dirty hands.   **3** He's got a dirty face.

1	2	3

4 Describing someone

10 Draw. Then write.

This is me.

My name's _____.

How old am I? I'm _____.

I've got _____ eyes and _____ hair.

Look at my favourite clothes.

I've got _____. I've got _____

_____ and I've got _____.

Pets

Animals / adjectives

1 Look and read. Then circle.

1 (parrot) / tortoise

2 hamster / cat

3 parrot / dog

4 frog / snake

5 tortoise / rabbit

6 mouse / frog

2 Read. Then draw.

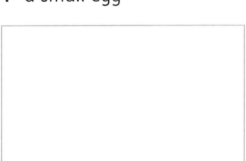

1 a small egg

2 a big goose

3 a short snake

4 a long snake

3 **Look and read. Then circle.**

1 What are (*that* / *those*)?

(*It's* / *They're*) frogs.

2 What (*is* / *are*) that?

(*It's* / *They're*) a rabbit.

3 What are (*that* / *those*)?

(*It's* / *They're*) mice.

4 **Write the question.**

1 What's _____?

It's a parrot.

2 _____?

They're snakes.

5 Unscramble and write.

you	Have	?	a	puppy	got

1 _____

I	.	haven't	,	No

2 _____

two	got	kittens	.	I've

3 _____

.	small	kittens	They're

4 _____

6 Unscramble. Then answer.

you rabbit Have a ? got

1 <u>Have you got a rabbit?</u> _____

✔ Yes, _____ .

got ? you Have tortoise a

2 _____

✗ _____ .

Has three he hamsters ? got

3 _____

✔ _____ .

she snake got Has a ?

4 _____

✗ _____ .

5 She's got a ...

7 Look. Then write (✔) or (✗).

	snake		
cat	dog	hamster	cat
dog	dog	tortoise	cat
Martha	**Tom**	**James and Liz**	**Sue**

1 Tom has got two dogs and a snake. ✔

2 Martha hasn't got a tortoise. She's got a hamster. ☐

3 James and Liz have got three pets. ☐

4 Sue's got two kittens. ☐

8 Look at Activity 5. Then answer.

1 Has Martha got a kitten? Yes, she _____.

2 Has James got a hamster and a dog? _____, _____.

3 Has Tom got two dogs? _____, _____.

4 Has Sue got a puppy? _____, _____.

9 **Look. Then read and match.**

My book of pets
Contents

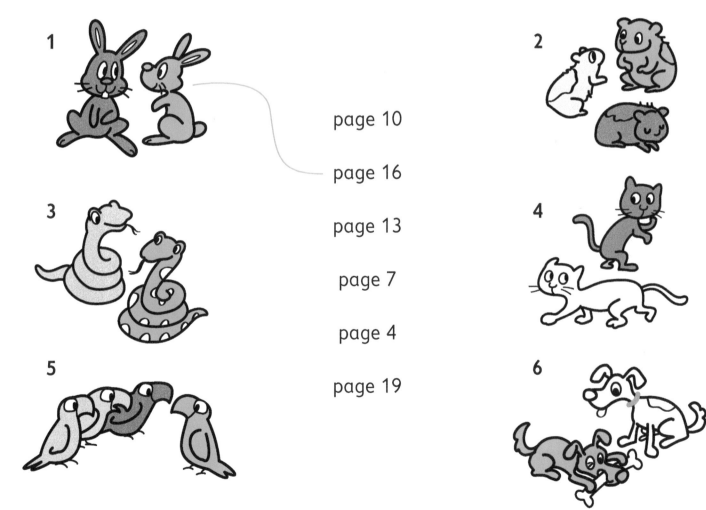

1

2

page 10

page 16

3

page 13

4

page 7

page 4

5

page 19

6

10 Match. Then write in alphabetical order.

1 h	ogs	<u>cats</u>
2 s	ats	_____
3 r	amsters	_____
4 d	arrots	_____
5 p	abbits	_____
6 c	nakes	_____

11 Make a pet book. Write the contents.

<u>My book of pets</u>

Animal   Page

<u>Cats</u>   page 1

_____   page 3

_____   page ___

_____   page ___

_____   page ___

My house

Rooms / furniture

1 Read. Then match.

a

1 garden

2 bathroom

3 kitchen

4 living room

b

c
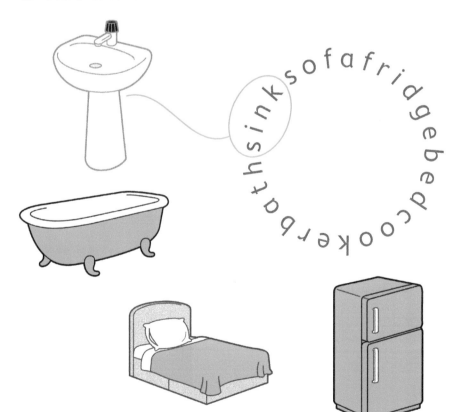

d

2 Find and circle. Then match.

sinksofafridgebedcookerbaths

6 Where's ...?

3 Look. Then write and circle.

Where ~~are~~ Granny Where

1 Where _____ are _____ Mum and Dad?

They're in the (garden / bathroom).

2 _____ is my sister?

She's in the (bathroom / bedroom).

3 Where are _____ and Grandad?

They're in the (living room / garden).

4 _____ is my brother?

He's in the (bedroom / kitchen).

4 Read. Then draw.

Living room

1 There's a dog under the lamp.

2 There's a sofa in the living room.

Kitchen

3 There's a cooker in the kitchen.

Bathroom

4 There's a sink under the window.

Bedroom

5 There are two kittens on the bed.

5 Follow. Then write.

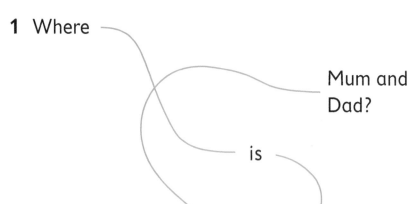

1 Where

2 Where

is

are

Mum and Dad?

Grandad?

They're in the _____.

Where is Grandad?

He's in the ___library___.

3 Where

4 Where

big

is

my

my

is

brother?

sister?

He's in the _____.

She's in the _____.

6 Read. Then draw.

1

This is my house. It's got four small windows and a big door. It's got a garden and three trees. There's a mouse in the garden. It's under a tree.

2

This is my house. It's got two small windows and a small door. It's got flowers in the garden. It's a small garden. I've got two dogs. Look! They are in the garden.

3

This is my flat. It's got three windows. It hasn't got a garden. It's got flowers under the windows. There are two flowers. Look! There's a bird on the flower under the window!

Remember!

Some words have the same sound but different spellings.

house and flower

7 **Write (✔) or (✗). Then correct.**

1 flowr ☒

flower

2 window ☐

3 howse ☐

4 gardin ☐

8 **Draw your favourite house. Then label. Use words from the box.**

living room   kitchen   bedroom   bathroom   window   door
bed   sink   cooker   garden   TV   sofa   lamp   bath

1 Read. Then circle the odd one out.

1 (cheese)   water   milk   juice

2 cheese   milk   yoghurt   meat

3 salad   carrots   fruit   fish

4 juice   jelly   water   juice

2 Read and draw. Then write.

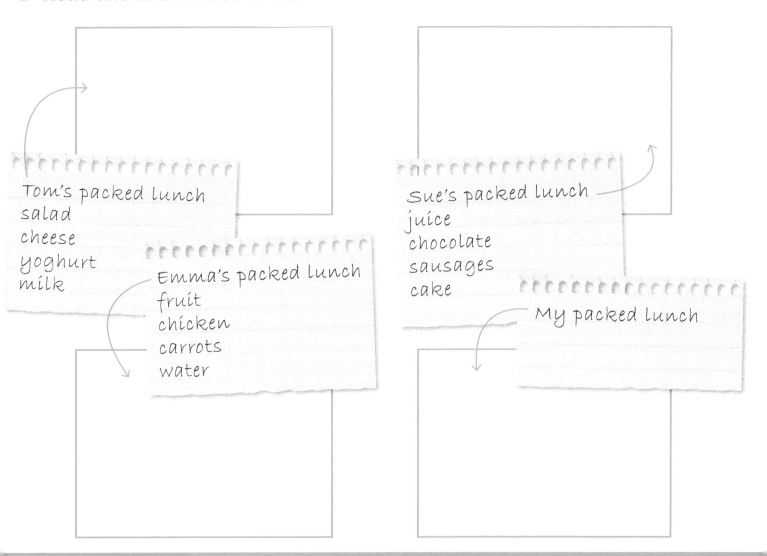

Tom's packed lunch
salad
cheese
yoghurt
milk

Emma's packed lunch
fruit
chicken
carrots
water

Sue's packed lunch
juice
chocolate
sausages
cake

My packed lunch

7 I like / don't like ...

3 Read and write (✔) or (✗). Then write.

1 chicken	✔	I ___like___ chicken.
2 yoghurt	☐	I _____ yoghurt.
3 fruit	☐	I _____ fruit.
4 milk	☐	I _____ milk.
5 cheese	☐	I _____ cheese.
6 salad	☐	I _____ salad.
7 bread	☐	I _____ bread.
8 juice	☐	I _____ juice.

4 Look at the table. Then write questions and answers.

	fruit	salad	meat
Mike	✔	✗	✔
Tracy	✗	✔	✔

Mike

_____ do you like?   I _____ fruit and meat.

I _____ like salad.

Tracy

What do you _____?   I like salad and _____.

I don't _____ fruit.

5 Complete the questions. Then circle your answers.

1

Do you
like vegetables?

2

_____
like jelly?

3

_____
like cake?

Yes, I do. / No, I don't.

Yes, I do. / No, I don't.

Yes, I do. / No, I don't.

6 Unscramble. Then answer.

| honey | Do | like | ? | you |

1 _____

_____

| ? | like | Do | you | water |

2 _____

_____

| chocolate | Do | ? | you | like |

3 _____

_____

7 Read and circle for you.

1 I (*like* / *don't like*) fruit.

2 I (*like* / *don't like*) vegetables.

3 I (*like* / *don't like*) cake.

4 I (*like* / *don't like*) jelly.

5 I (*like* / *don't like*) meat.

8 Read. Then write sentences.

carrots   juice   chocolate   sandwich
water   salad   ice cream

I like
I don't like

1 carrots   I like carrots.

2 juice   _____

3 chocolate   _____

4 sandwich   _____

5 water   _____

6 salad   _____

7 ice cream   _____

9 Read. Then write (✔) or (✘) for Rita.

What food do you like, Rita?
Do you like salad?

No, I don't.

Do you like chicken?

No, I don't.

Do you like fruit?

No, I don't.

What food do you like?

I like cake, chocolate, ice cream and sweets ...

Wow! That's all bad for you!!!!!

Questionnaire   <u>Rita</u>

Do you like salad?

Do you like fruit?

Do you like chicken?

Do you like ice cream?

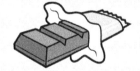

7 A questionnaire

10 Find the mistakes. Read and write (✔) or (✗). Then correct.

1 Do you like sausages. ✗ Do you like sausages? _____

2 Do you like yoghurt? ☐ _____

3 I like chips? ☐ _____

4 Yes, I do. ☐ _____

5 No, I don't? ☐ _____

6 I don't like carrots. ☐ _____

11 Write. Then draw.

Questionnaire

Do you like ___milk___ ?

Do you like _____ ?

Do you _____ ?

_____

I'm happy

Are you hungry?

1 **Look. Then write. Use the words from the box.**

| happy   thirsty   tired   hungry |

1

2

3

4

_____   _____   _____   _____

2 **Look, read and match.**

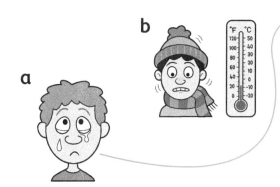

b

a

1 sad

2 cold

3 hot

4 ill

5 hurt

6 angry

7 bored

c

d

e

f

g

3 Follow. Write the questions and answers.

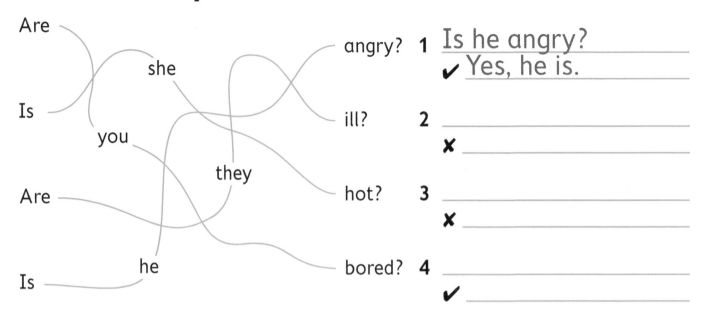

Are

she

Is

you

they

Are

he

Is

angry? **1** Is he angry?
✔ Yes, he is.

ill? **2** _____
✗ _____

hot? **3** _____
✗ _____

bored? **4** _____
✔ _____

4 Use words from the box and write. Then draw.

hurt   happy   hot   hungry

I'm _____ .

He's _____ .

She's _____ .

They're _____ .

5 Read and match. Then write and draw.

1 There's a spider under my bed.

a _____ thirsty!

2 This is my brother. He likes chips.

b _I'm_ scared!

3 This is my Mum. It's her birthday today.

c _____ happy!

4 I like juice.

d _____ hungry!

6 Read, choose and write.

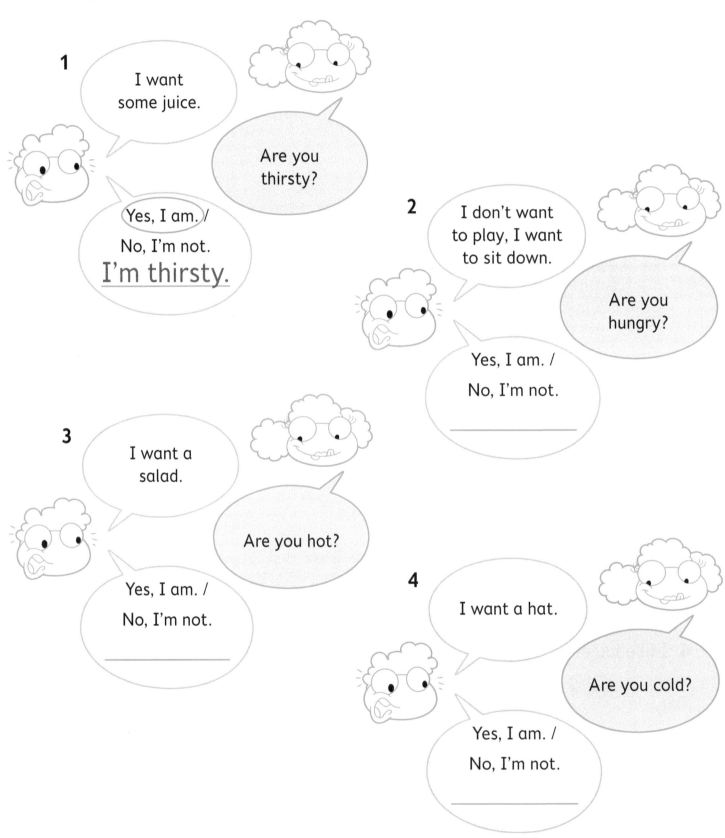

1

I want some juice.

Are you thirsty?

Yes, I am. / No, I'm not.
I'm thirsty.

2

I don't want to play, I want to sit down.

Are you hungry?

Yes, I am. / No, I'm not.
_____

3

I want a salad.

Are you hot?

Yes, I am. / No, I'm not.
_____

4

I want a hat.

Are you cold?

Yes, I am. / No, I'm not.
_____

7 Read the headlines. Then match.

Tom, Kate, Emma and Ben are in the park.

1 **Tom's happy**

2 **Emma's bored**

3 **Ben's angry**

4 **Kate's happy**

a 4

Kate has got Ben's toy car.
Kate wants a toy car for her birthday.
'This is my favourite toy. I like cars.'

b ☐

Kate has got Ben's toy car.
Ben wants it. 'It's my car, Kate!'

c ☐

Emma hasn't got a car.
She's got a ball.

d ☐

It's Tom's birthday. He's in the park.
He's got a bike.
'Look at my new bike!'

8 I'm happy!

Remember!

I've **got** = I **have got**

I'm = I **am**

it's = **it** is

8 **Read. Write a headline. Then trace and colour.**

happy   bored   hungry

I'm happy.

It's carnival time!
I've got a mask.
It's a butterfly mask.
It's red and green.

I'm _____

I'm in my kitchen.
I like vegetables and fish.
I like chocolate and fruit!
I like food!

I'm _____

My friends are in the garden.
I'm in bed. I'm ill.
I want to play.